See Me - Hear Me

COME - LOOK - SEE -

- I AM ME -

Trish Milne

YOUR MENTAL HEALTH MATTERS

Presentation by *BookLeaf Publishing*

Web: www.bookleafpub.com

E-mail: info@bookleafpub.com

ISBN: 9789358737684

First edition 2023

I dedicate this work to my boys, David and Logan.

I may have birthed them but it was them that gave me life.

My two miracles, both strong in their own way

Always loved.

Mum.

To my Josh, your light will always shine bright

Always in my heart

Rest In Peace buddy

Love

Auntie Trish

ACKNOWLEDGEMENT

Alan, for being the most solid support ever, my emotional support monkey; love you always.
To my girls, you know who you are :) who witnessed and also spoke out, also punished; we've got this, true friendships never fade; we just get happier.
Linda Crockett, an amazing woman and counsellor, so happy Al found her when he did. Specialist in Workplace Harassment, Bullying and Violence Situations, a shining star.
Allowed me to talk, helping me to leave some dark places behind.
To Mike who just let me prattle on every week - love ya.

PREFACE

In a workplace where it is unsafe to disagree, it is not a place of learning but an environment of control.
Once reported to the appropriate people it only got worse.
Cronyism and nepotism is rife and it starts from the top.
When you do not comply, you are punished.
Be Strong - Be Seen - Be Heard
This is not a victim mindset,
I was not a victim -
I was a TARGET!

Many others are targeted and dismissed
Far too many people falling ill
We should not be tolerating this conduct.
Your workplace should be a safe space.
I can assure you nothing was confidential with anything I reported, the powers that be made sure of that.
They made my life a living hell.
I was the only one that remained silent.

NO MORE, NOT EVER, NO MORE

STAND UP AND BE COUNTED

WHY?

Not once did you ever think you'd be here,
dreading your work and living in fear
To be silenced, ostracised, gas-lighted, unfair,
to be targeted daily by them all, a nightmare.

She taught them by example
how to treat you that way
You tried to speak up
that made it worse, I did say.

The ones who had the power
tried to hide it from all
Protected the abusers,
tripped you up, made you fall
They lied, they gossiped, you never felt safe
you needed to get to a different place.

The others got turned to work against you
to keep you in line for them all to see,

the fear of losing their jobs was what it took
The damage they could do,
they just needed them to look.

The fear, the coercion, the power at play
Don't ever speak out as they'll make sure you
pay.
Your mind then plays tricks
you're then doubting yourself,
So they play with your mind, your fears, you fall
ill.
It's a game that they play
they draw it out for so long,
to make you believe that you
do not belong.

They hit you mentally, physically, and
financially too
they want you to know that they'll destroy you.
You start to believe that you are going mad.
life just becomes so terribly bad.

You're forced to the point
where you can't take no more,
You start destroying yourself -
numb to the core.
It's the wrong thing to do
I'll just let you know,
these people don't care

You've gotta grow.

You struggle to find the help that you need
to tell your story and for you all to read,
There is a way out, you've got to stand strong
And believe in yourself as you did nothing
wrong.

That the truth shall push through for me and for
you
and life is worth living, we know to be true,
that strong people we need to make this alright
will take on these injustices -
and continue the fight.

For the rights of us all

YOU SEE

I'm in this living hell

You see -

The damage that you've done
The pleasure that you took from it
Can never be un-done.

You see -

Hell will take you in its arms
You never will escape
Death will take you slowly dear
Not for you those Pearly Gates

You see-

Karma has this way you know
To punish evil as it is
Enjoy the way you are going my dear
With the devil's deadly kiss.

Karma is the most patient of assassins -
ENJOY -

THE FOOL

She will get what she wants
No matter if it's wrong.
She will love bomb, destroy
And hate you all along.

When she opens her mouth
It's just lie after lie,
But you will not beat her
(that's what she thinks)
No matter how you try.

She will name drop, intimidate til she gets her
own way,

Turn others against you - cos that's how she
plays.
It's all about her, not about you
She continues to lie so she can get by.

She's nasty and cruel but the world cannot know
She's got an image to keep and you all to
control.
The Chess Player, his snakes, HR in the mix -
You're weak in her eyes as she plays all her
tricks.

Target after target
She doesn't care
Don't cry at her
Just because she ain't fair.

No-one must know as she cannot show -
The evil malignant scum that she is,
Or her game is up
before it truly begins.

No-one has ever said NO to her

Pure Evil

TEFLON

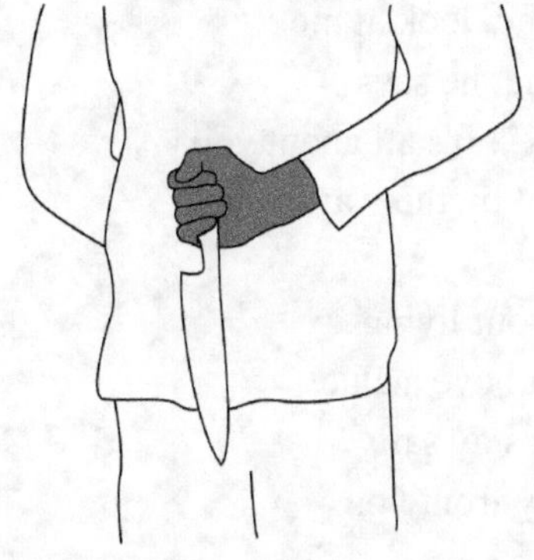

In the body of a boy
and the mind of a bitch
He will gossip and lie
He's no more than a snitch.

A buddy to all -
- but a real friend to none
Worse than the worst
He's nothing but scum.

Room to room he goes
Spreading his lies
He hated on me
I saw through his disguise.

Pity no one else can!!
Or can they -
But they don't wanna see

Or they will get treated the same way as me.

Look at me, look at me
That's what he says
You think .. It's all about you
No it's not by the way!!

Life is about living
You don't have a clue
I've gotta stay safe
well away from you

Rotten to the core.

TEFLON AND THE FOOL

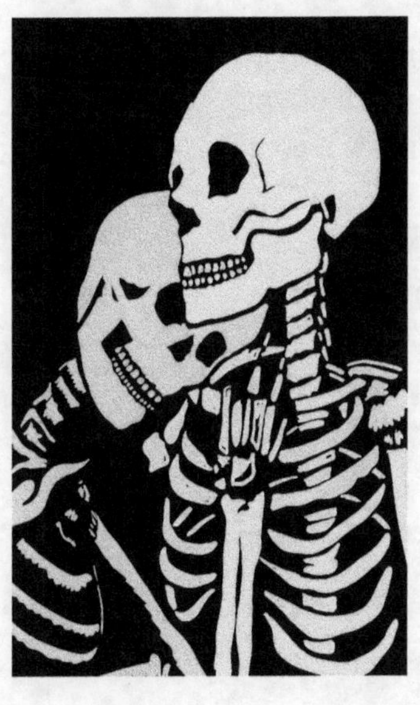

Part 1

Like two leeches
Feeding off each other
At a dead man's party.

Latch on

Part 2

Two malignant narcissists
Who played all of you
You never saw it coming
I did!!

Eyes open

THE CHESS PLAYER- PART 1 AND PART 2

You position your buddies all around you,
Keeping you safe, controlling your crew.
You have the power to stop this
You weak, feeble man
You choose to let it carry on
Just because you can.

Move after move, you keep them running
Mobbing, Intimidation, Harassment Techniques.
You keep it coming.
Cronyism, nepotism, round and round it goes
Keep yourself hidden but control the moves
And that now truly shows

You are a snivelling human being
And now we are all seeing,
All the moves you will use
To enhance the abuse.

Snakes and Ladders

Part 2

The first words out of your mouth -
I will not tolerate bullying
YOU LIED
You allow it to happen -
When it's you and your cronies leading the pack.

Disgraceful behaviour

BLIND EYES

Because of you all choosing to say you never
saw
Even when you did see!
I nearly died - as your lack of action is
what nearly killed me.

Mouths can lie, eyes cannot,
People may forget,
Karma will not.

Neither will God by the way

TEFLON, THE FOOL, NOW ADDING THE TOOL

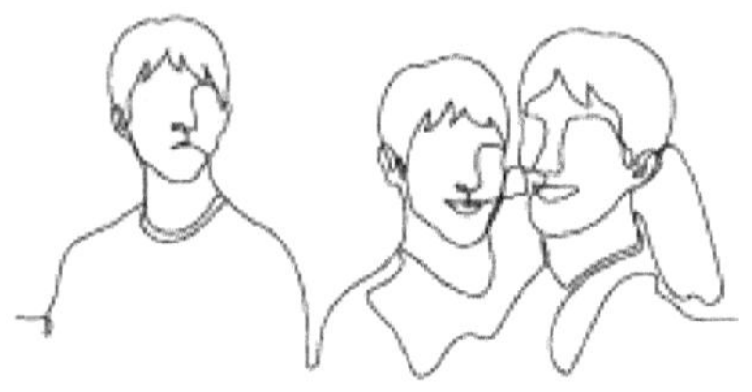

When you first came on board
A friend of my family
I helped you set up, just like I do
Well - that all changed when
You joined the Devil's crew

You Tool

You targeted me relentlessly
I was so totally confused
How could you do this to me daily
I believed you were being used.

You Tool

The depths of depravity you went to
To make my life hurt more
You smirked, you laughed, you enjoyed it
Like you were keeping score.

You are a sick individual!!
You knew that you were safe
As The Fool and Teflon needed me
To be in a dark and lonely place.

You Tool

I tried and tried, you exhausted me out
You pointed, you sneered, you towered over me.
Threatening behaviour, you knew you harmed
me
Many people saw it but chose not to see!!

You Tool

So I took myself home and I started to pray
Come on baby girl, you'll have your say
DO NOT, DO NOT, END YOUR OWN LIFE.
They're not worth it I said as I held onto that
knife…

TIGHTLY!!

You Tool

I want you to know, that no matter what
That Teflon and The Fool used you -

AS THEIR TOOL,

To destroy me you see was always their plan
You're just their plaything, their toy
You're sure not a man.

YOU TOOL

Think for yourself you manufactured puppet

THE SNAKES - 1 AND 2

Slither out of the darkness
And face what you've done
The pleasure you took in my suffering
Was second to none.

The smirk on your face
And the joy in your eyes
When you watched me break down -
when tears flowed with my cries.

Now the world's gonna know that
You truly are - The lowest of the low.
The chess player should really
 have just let this snake go.

There's trouble ahead
And I've played fair,
I smell your fear
Like blood in the air.

When you look in the mirror
Are there scales on your face
Let me tell you this- snake -
I'm in this world. . for the longest race.

A snake only sheds its skin to become a bigger
snake.

Snake no.2

A female one this time, no fear
No different from the male.
Her forked tongue flickers back and fore
Just to let you know the score.

She allowed this to continue on
This assault on me - too long
each time we spoke, your lies just grew
You snake, I can't trust you.

You are a power-hungry, greedy little soul

Being top dog is your only goal.

Were you cornered by The Chess Player?
Were you told to play a game?
Downplay the truth I told you
To make me out to be insane.

I told you the truth, it hurt your heart
You lied to me, it was just your act!!

God have mercy on your soul
That's if he can find it.

Lost Soul

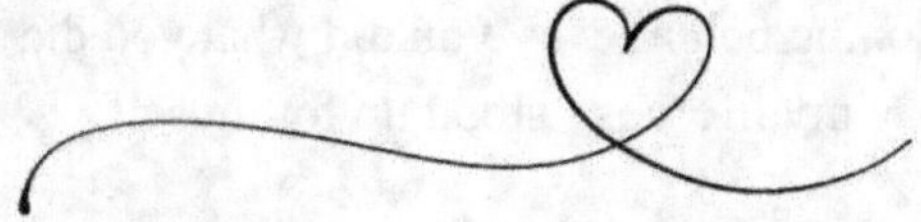

THE BATTLE INSIDE MY HEAD

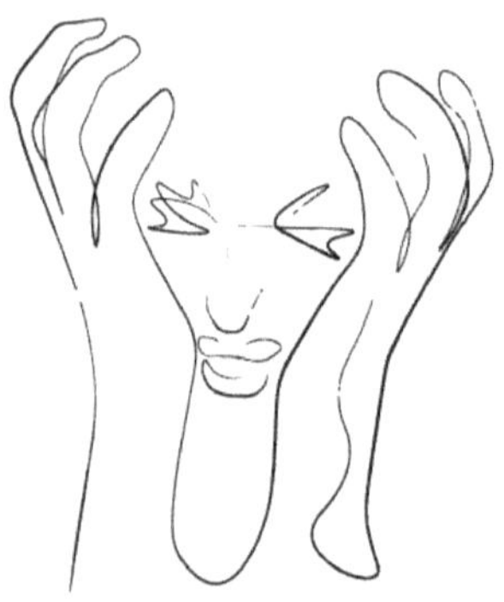

The darkness, despair, the fight in my mind.
Daily thoughts of suicide and for what ----- I
can not find
The reasoning behind why you did what you did
To destroy my life 'cos I stood up for myself.

To stop bullying, harassment was all that I tried
You hid behind your egos, you're fake, I just
cried.!!!
Your friends in high places protecting all you
Everyone denied what you knew to be true.

Flying monkeys around for the likes of you.
Gossip can kill
You kill, you kill
But fighting on is all I can do

To let the world know - all about you!!

The battle never ends
Round and round we all go
You will not stop me
I will be heard!!

To save any other person who has suffered like
this
For me to stand up, let this be known
I will fight on - my mind has just grown
I promise you this - the truth will come out!!!

With a loving family around me
And real friends - so true
A counsellor who listens - I will get through.
To save our society we need help from above
This world needs to know the true meaning of
LOVE.

End the Stigma

This is my story as I live it

HEAVEN AND HELL

My father has just said to me
No pearly gates for you
He's locked them so securely
Heaven's not here . . .
for the devil's crew.

Gates closed

There's a Highway to Hell he told me
And you're all heading down that way
You all sold your souls to the devil
And now it's time for you to pay

No coming back

SEE ME

You all saw what was happening
Some took pleasure joining in
You even turned your backs on me
Oh, where do I begin . . . .

What did I ever do to you
You joined in with their lies
You made my life a living hell
You even heard my cries.

Only one of you would help me
Then you all turned on her too
And that woman had integrity
So your hatred carried on through.

The Fool and Teflon gossipped

You joined in with gossip too
Like good children you'd just tow the line
Or they would get to you.

You gave them so much power
And they also knew that too
Because you turned a blind eye
Their power grew and grew.

They'll always need a target
You better pray it is not you
Because everyone you work with
Will also target you.

Eyes wide shut

YOUR CHOICE

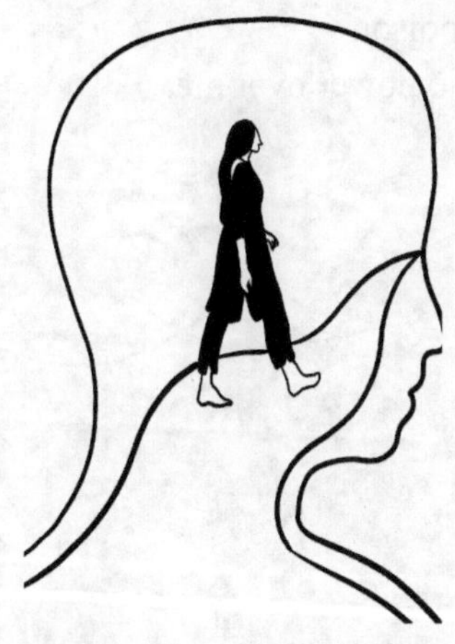

Set my mind free
For the whole world to see
To hear my words
As that will be me

See into my mind
But please be kind
It's a messed up place
and that's no disgrace

The damage has been done
But I will overcome
Hear me, feel me,
live me, love me

Fear me, hate me -
- that one's on you!!

Pick your poison
You hold no power over me.

THANK YOU

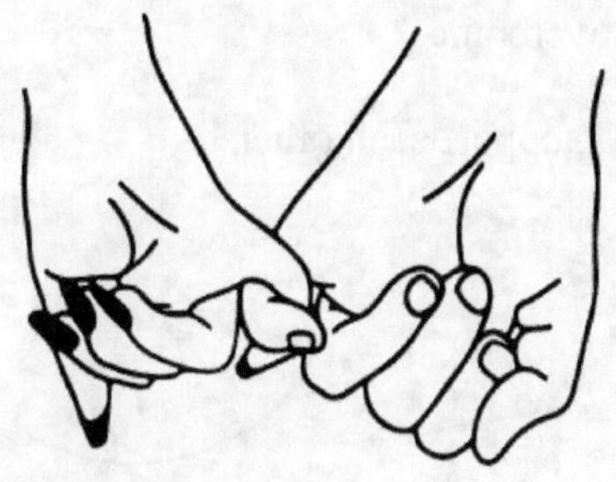

To the ones that stayed with me
throughout
There weren't very many but I think we
got it right,
you will never truly understand
the wealth of love you gave
helped me so much,
in you I trust,
my life you helped to save.

You make this world a better place
you suffered with me too
I'm sorry that this happened
But true friendship shone right through.

We dealt, we lived, we grew so much,
Hard times but we still thrive
we just proved that all we need
was real love for us to survive.

Let them weave their wicked ways

Our days with them are done
When we find our strength within
We will overcome.

Love and support each other.

DIALECT

My dialect is not derogatory,
It is part of who I am
You must have been giddy with power
To put that one in your plan.

YOU FOOL

The fibs you must have told
for them to agree with you
Your lies and lies just grew
So they (once again) just covered you.

YOU FOOL

But this is the part that we all want to see
For on the video call they apologised to me.
They got it wrong they said, they took you at
your word
Your word means nothing and that is what I
heard.

You lied

YOU FOOL

How dare I speak the way I do
Why can't I talk this way?
You don't like how I pronounce my words
so I'll never have a say!!

YOU FOOL

Oh no you won't, you can't stop me
my dialect is mine
I'll take my words and speak the truth
and I will be just fine.

I am me
I AM ME

DO I CARE

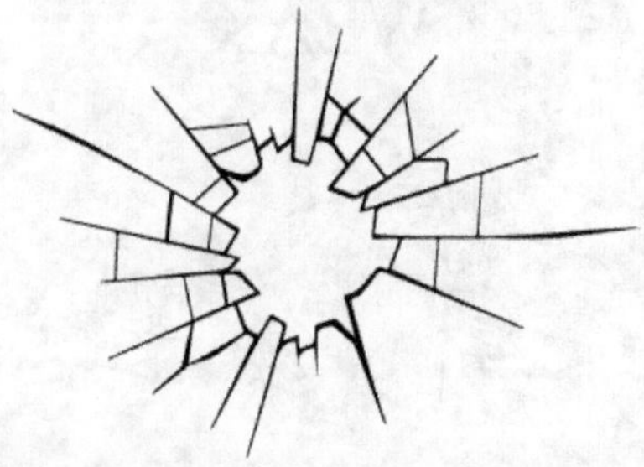

I cared about everything but not anymore,
I feel nothing at all now
I'm empty and cold.
The damage has taken me and I -
do not care.

I'm numb to the core -
No happiness -
No love -
No friendships -
No fear.

Am I insane - so I don't feel the pain
No reason to live
Goodbye
Til we meet again.

Help

STRONG - BUT SO - WEAK

You saw what the tool
Did to me every single day,
I get that your job was important to you
But you should have held onto integrity.
You chose not to
So I will have my say . . .

We talked, we laughed, we spoke about life,
You were part of my day and I felt no strife,
But walking away so they'd leave you alone
Hurt me so much but I should have known.

You left me to be targeted day after day,
But that could have stopped
If you had stood up to say
Enough, no more, this is wrong by the way
BUT YOU DID NOT

You weak individual

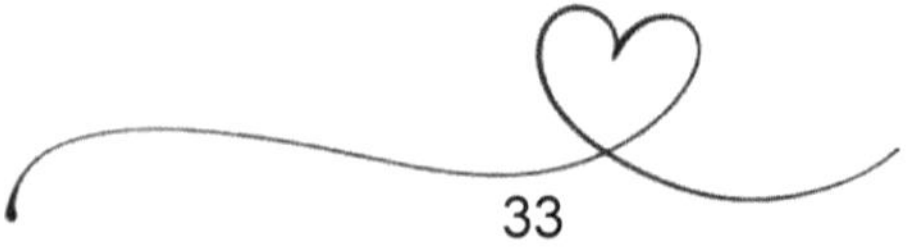

FEELING

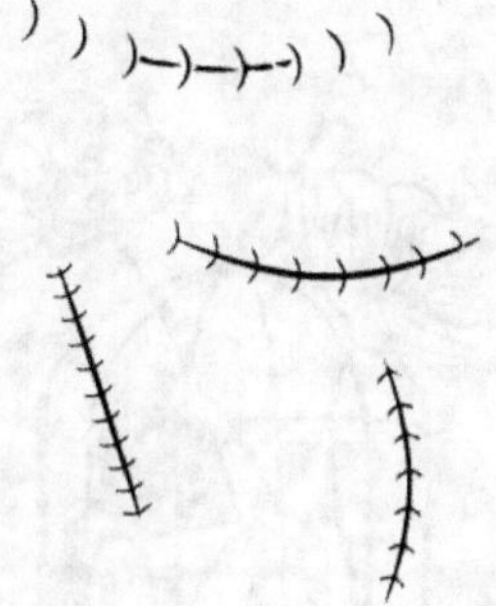

Scratch, scratch, scratch, scratch,
Cut, cut, cut.

Places no one ever sees
My hands and face so clear
Never below my elbows, never below my knees
Let me feel something . . . please.

Just let me be me
Let me feel that blood trickle
I just want to feel free

Cut, cut, cut, cut
But no one ever sees!!

Feel something

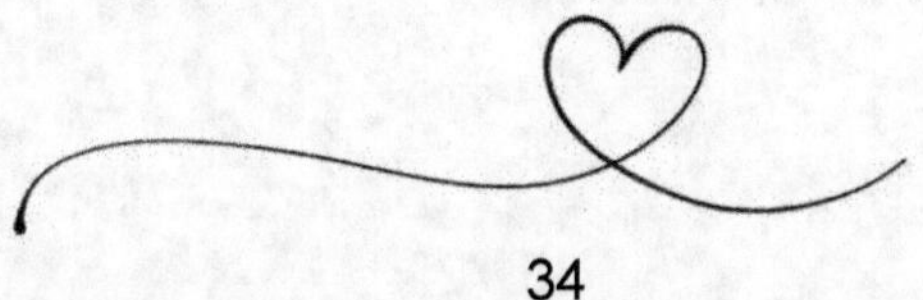

HORTON HEARS A WHAT!!

Does he have you running . . .

to help the division hide the abuse
A game for all of you to play
To blame, humiliate, destroy me
just to stop me having my say . . .

NO WAY!!

That's not going to happen
No way, not now, not ever
You can all label me mad, insane,
not right . . but whatever

We all know exactly what happened
And we can all make a choice
The truth never changes
You will all hear my voice!!

I have nightmares you see
Every day of my life

The damage inflicted can not be undone
You played games with my mind
And still I can't find . . the reasoning on why
You thought that was fun

You just created a loaded gun

Shots fired

A fragment of myself still fighting the good
fight,
diminish my brightness, fading, fading . . .
almost done
No way, stay strong, hold onto one more night
Stand firm, believe and I shall overcome

You watched me cry throughout this process
You didn't care at all

Your job was to discredit me
To see how hard I'd fall.

You retired, took your place on the board
The chess player's mouthpiece (so it is told)
Your soul's already sold
To the highest bidder . . your blood just runs ice
cold.

You pawn

SET ME FREE

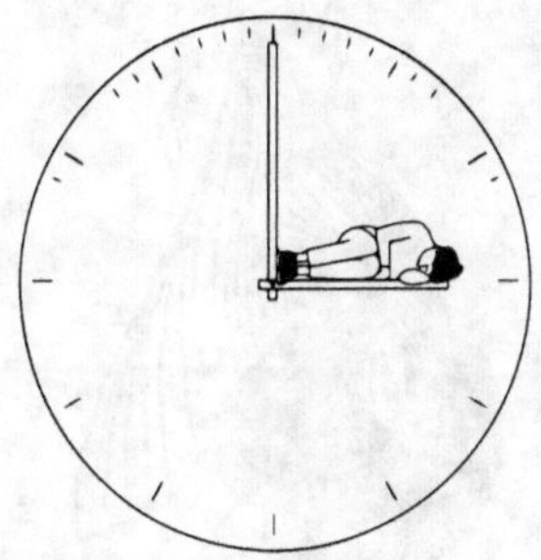

Tick, Tock, Tick, Tock,
The madness in my mind
Tick, Tock, Tick, Tock
Let's see what we can find
Tick, Tock, Tick, Tock
I am a loaded gun
Tick, Tock, Tick, Tock
Just look at what you've done!!
Tick, Tock, Tick, Tock
Death has me on my knees
Tick, Tock, Tick, Tock
Shots fired - I do not freeze.

Bang

INNOCENCE

I will bring you to your knees
She said
My crazy messed up mind
That innocence you're looking for
But you will never find
It's hidden deep inside of you
I will keep it well locked up,
Keep searching dear - but you will fear -
The day you do
It's up to you
It is safe - and in its place
Well away from you.

Menace in My Mind

REMAINING SILENT

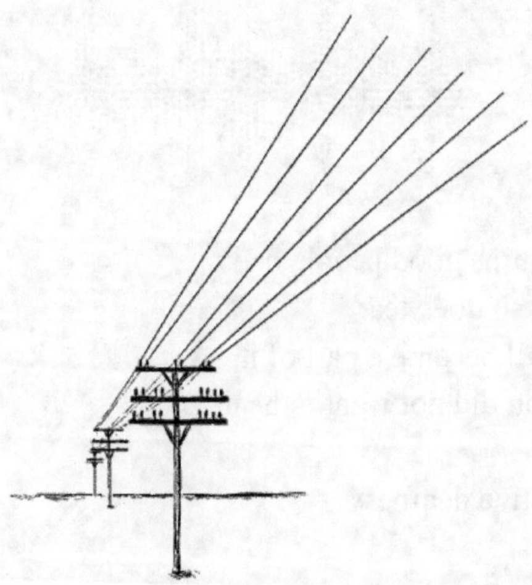

Keeping silent about the abuse that you saw,
Encouraged the abusers to give it their all
We suffered because you never stood up
You made it harder for us -
- but you all made your call.

SILENCE IS PARTICIPATION

HEAR ME

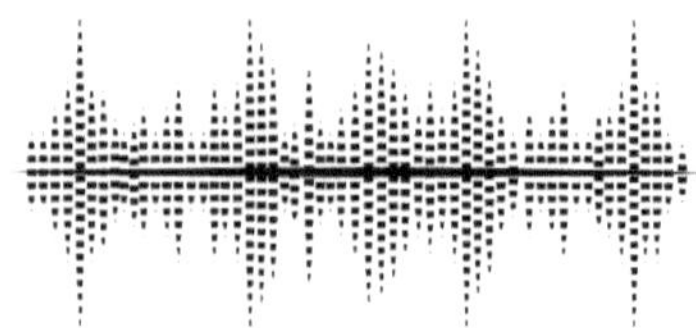

Evil turns good people bad
Also, so does fear
You all became a part of it
As you did not want to hear

Selective deafness

PARANOIA

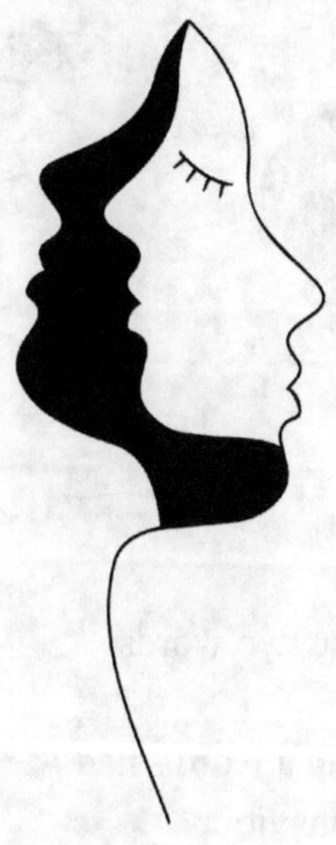

Is it paranoia if it's the truth?
Asking for a friend.

Valid question

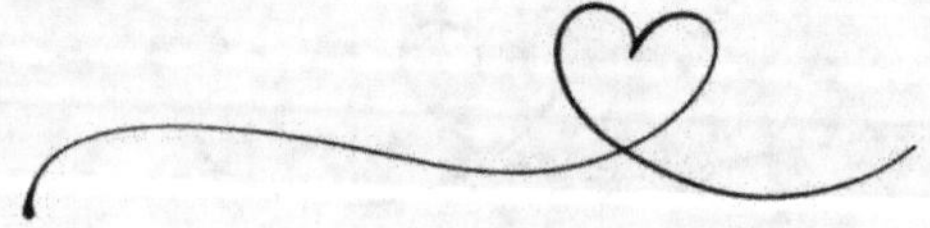

I'M SO, SO, SORRY

You know those two words
I'M SORRY
Just mixed up in a word salad
No changed behaviour
WELL . .
That's not an apology -
That's manipulation.

You Tool

THE SCHOOL WITH A HEART

- Only Joking

They talk about supporting Victim Services
It truly does depend on who the victim is.
If it doesn't fit their deeds
It will never fit their needs.
You are alone!!

NO HEART AT ALL

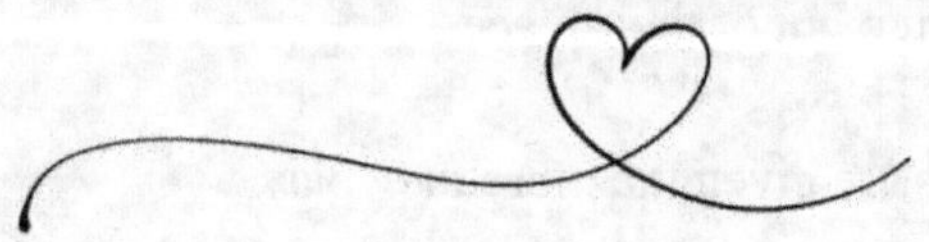

FLYING MONKEYS

What's worse than a narcissist?
It's their flying monkeys of course
They encourage them to do what they do!
Defend them, so they come after you.

They feed them to protect themselves
Lie for them to feel safe
They also know that they will turn on them
If they step out of their place.

Rewards are given the more they play
The more you suffer, the higher the pay,
I am stronger than those monkeys

I will hold on to the truth
These are educated people
But oh my- just so uncouth!!

Keep flying under the radar to keep yourselves
safe!!

Poisonous hearts

NARCISSISTS

Narcissists are charming
As charm is the highest form
Of manipulation.
Do you see how they play?
Stay clear of them all
Or they will enjoy watching you fall.

Scum.

GRAB - LET GO

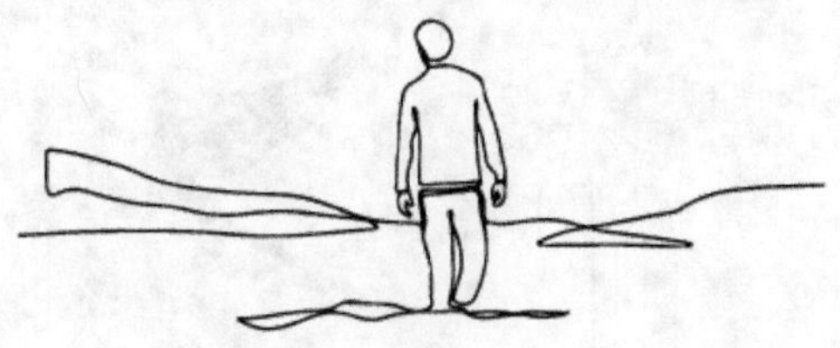

I first met you on video call
You listened to me-
in utter shock
The true story I had told you
Had you sitting between a hard place
- and a rock.

I had you on the edge . . .
And then you made this pledge -

HAHA

No matter where they put me
I will see this through - no fear
That was a lie, and shame on you
You did not reappear.

Did you think the end of the meeting was it?
You truly make me sick!!

Keep on hiding

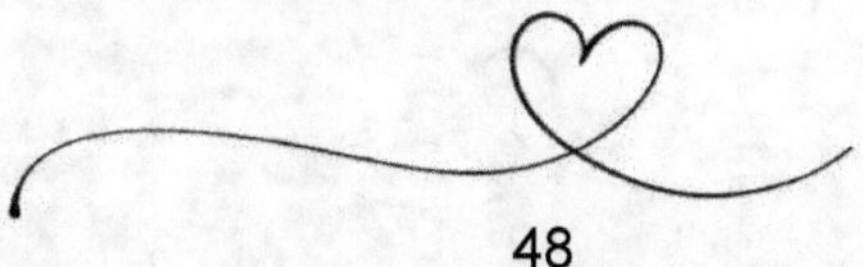

ALL THE ABUSE

A union, nothing more
They paid for your service
Enablers to the core
You never did care for the truth to be told
You attacked, you intimidated -
Your integrity has been sold

You kept dragging it out
Nothing safe in your hands
Keeping your heads buried
Deep into the sands.

Keep hiding, keep lying
I really don't care
I will keep living
Head held high in the air.

Standing Tall - Middle Finger To You All

RECENCY BIAS

Teflon used recency bias like it's
his own personal get-out clause
Whenever he was called out on anything,
Then he would just pause

Out he came, timing it so well
Parents watching, so close to the bell
He's playing a game with you all
He's winning it too
It's called covering his tracks
He doesn't care about you.

To be seen, to be seen, it's all about him

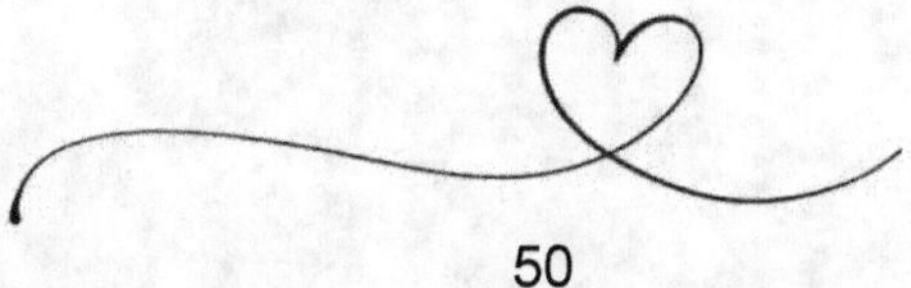

MUSICAL NOTES

In and out she weaves about
Like musical notes just dancing around
Spreading gossip, lies, encouraging them all
Waiting for you to call

She's gonna have a long wait.

NO FRIEND AT ALL

CHUCK A CHUCK

Not the smartest by far
Just a thug in jeans
Throw a ball at our faces again
I DARE YA

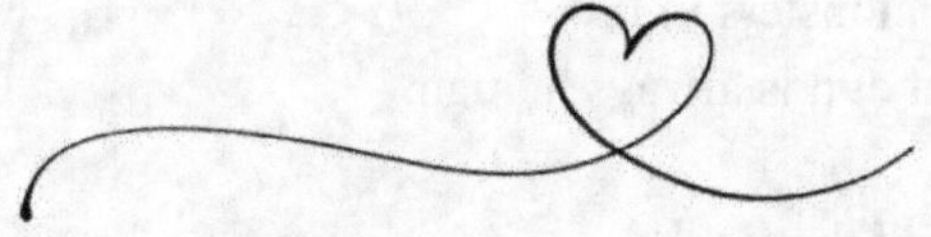

MONSTERS/EVIL

Scooby Doo taught me
that it is people who are indeed
the real monsters in life
And that evil is always human.

Now, ain't that sad!!

THE BOARD - I'M BORED

Flat out, straight out
On the level, never
Pieces for The Chess Player
Tell the truth, no, not ever

Cover their tracks
Protect the abusers
Powers given to them all.
They're not there to protect the kids
Or the parents, that's for sure
You've gotta get rid of all of them
As that's the only reasonable cure.

They are there to feed their own
Their families, their friends
That's what I mean.
Hugs to the antagonists
(Dates Saved)
From my own eyes that was seen.

Cronyism at its worst (or best)
Depending on who you are

They've all got a job to do
And it's not to look after you.

Just have a look at who's on the board
It isn't hard to see
It's all a game they like to play.
Power hungry, protected
Now that is the key

Unlock and see for yourself

RED FLAGS

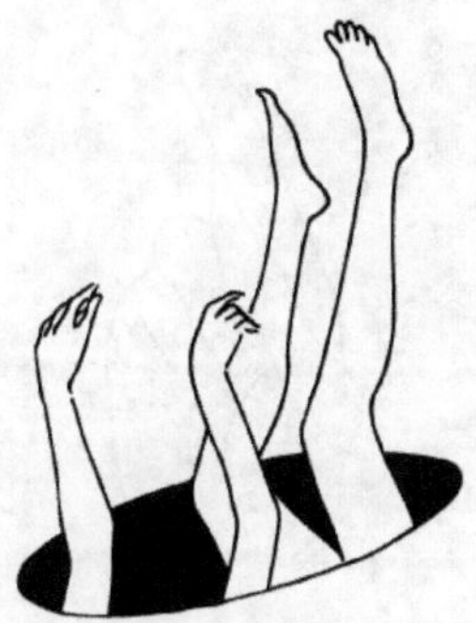

Waving, flying, all around
Those flags that are blood red
Should have gone with my gut instinct
But instead I went with my head.

Never again, that messed me up
I wished I could not see
This dangerous game they played
was all about them
It was never about you or me.

They have got away with this for years.

Gut instinct wins from now on.

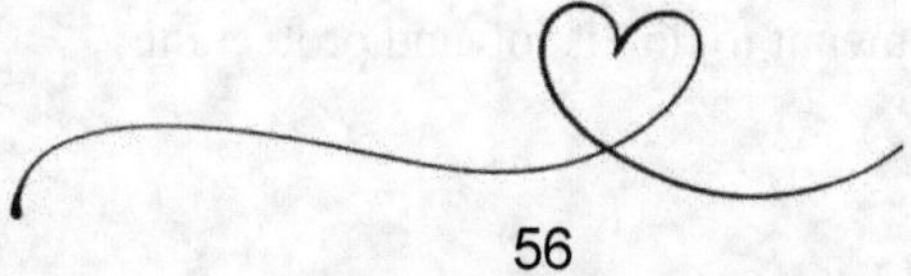

BOUNDARIES

I set myself the boundaries
To keep myself safe at work.
No-one had ever done this to you
The contempt in your eyes told me
That danger for me was about to ensue

The audacity of me to call you out
Who did I think I was
Your gaslighting techniques ramped up
More damage to me you'd cause.

I did report this to the Principal
That was one of my first mistakes
How was I supposed to know
That you and him were such good mates.

He was meant to do his job and protect me

HE DID NOT

How did he put it, oh yeah, it had nothing to do
with him.

FEELING UNSAFE

Your workplace should be a safe space
Sadly for some, it is not.
It can be brutal and nasty
Your downfall they will plot.

They call themselves a family
It's a messed up one for sure.
Do as they say or you will pay
Or daily injustices you will endure.

The black sheep of the family
The ones who see through it all
Your games we will not play
And definitely won't do as you say.

You are wrong on so many levels
God forgive you cos we won't.
Forced out of our jobs that we loved
Because of cruelty and lies
that we exposed.

Let's bring this into the open
To take the power away from you
Black sheep we may be
And I will always be me
I'm up for the fight now . .
Let's allow the whole world to see.

Hospitalized by the actions of the work family . .
so wrong

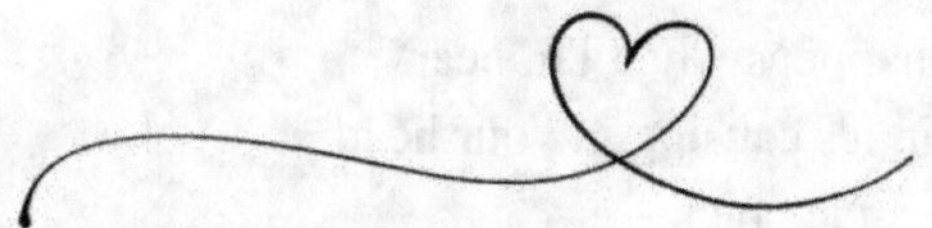

ICE PICK

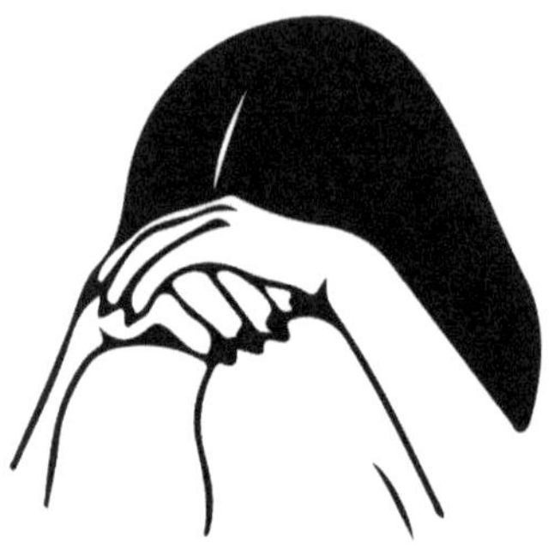

I'm waiting at my bus line
And what do we all hear,
You strutting down the pathway -
Shouting out - you made this clear -

Oh, what's that noise, oh
What's that noise?
It only happens when I'm near.
The pain it's causing in your head
It's like an ice pick -
to the back of your ear.

It's when I speak, you told me
My voice, it causes you pain.
I looked you in the eye and asked
Are you starting on me again?

Were you playing that character in Pig Girl
Robert Pickton was his name,
You said no, I wasn't sure
I went home and vomited again.

You played your part in gaslighting me
You're disgusting, stay away
An educator/councillor acting that way
Shame on you, I say!!
You snorted at me - you pig.

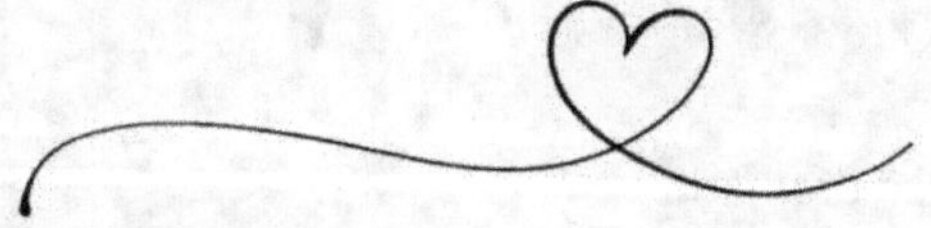

GASLIGHTING

You're so dramatic -
-No I am not
You sound so crazy -
-No I do not
That didn't happen -
-Yes it did, we all saw
Stop feeling sorry for yourself -
-I never did, not at all.

It's not a big deal -
-Yes it was by the way
You're remembering things wrong -
-No I'm not, I would say.
We were just joking -
-Well that joke was on me.

We wouldn't have done that to you -
-Yep you did, you made me pay.

Why are you still here if it's so bad -
-I loved my job but it has now made me sad.
You're imagining things, it's all in your head -
-You all wore me down, I felt dead.
You need help -
-I didn't but now that part is true.

That's what gaslighting sounds like, day in, day
out
It's going to affect you, one way or the other,
it's dangerous mind games
But they'll say - you're just too emotional.

Mind Blown

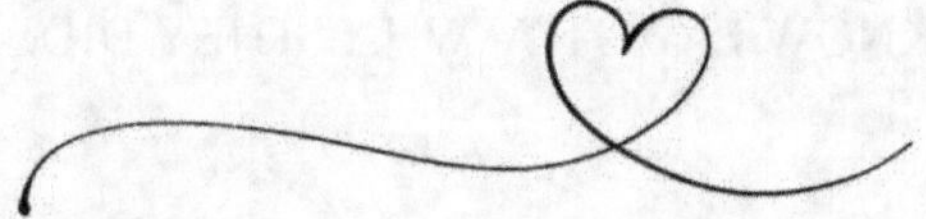

MENTAL HEALTH

They promote themselves as being mental health
aware.
I have not been at work for over a year.
And no-one from any level of this organisation
Has checked in on me
NOW - that really says it all.

THEY KNOW EXACTLY WHAT THEY DID.

THE GOOD AROUND US ALL

No matter what you've been through,
Some days it can be bad.
Just remember there are good things
In this world that can be had.

Set yourself some projects
Getting out of bed is one
There are miracles all around us
And just remember you are one.

Surround yourself with the people you trust
A small crew is all you need
They will lift you up and hold you strong
Allow you to believe that you do belong.

Happiness, love, fun times we all need

And these people will help plant that seed
That the world needs you and all you give
that kindness and happiness is the way to live.

Butterflies and rainbows

LOVING

Loving and living your best life
Is the way to go
Don't ever forget your past
But don't dwell there,
that's a no.

Get out and feel that wind in your hair
Get your hands dirty, seeds to sow
Bring forth your sunshine and the rain,
Yourself and the plants, you need to grow

To take that pain away - to begin again.

Get me my net

I'm away out to catch the wind
(quote by a 4yr old Logan)

Don't ever forget the good in the world

I'M BACK

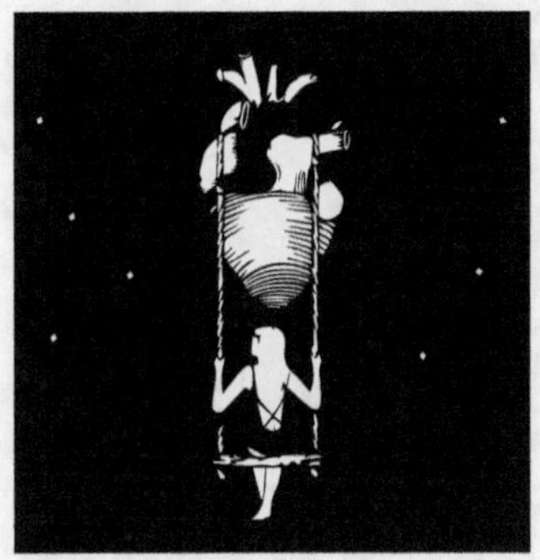

I am refusing to dim my light
For you to feel better about yourself
I refuse to lower my work standards
Just because you won't raise yours.

I will continue to support and spread love
around me
Because that's my style and it brings happiness,
you see.
I'm full of giggles, just bursting with joy
And that is something you cannot destroy.

Peace out

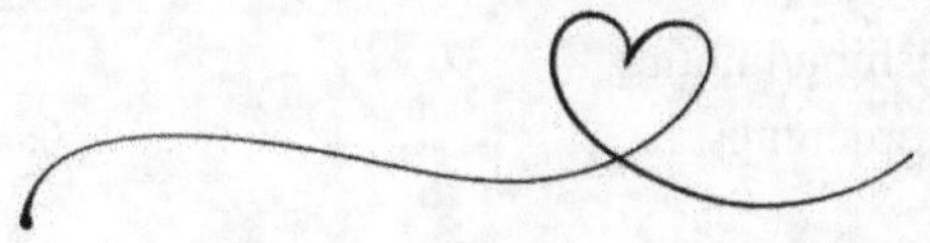

JOURNEY

I hope you've enjoyed this journey with me
This has been part of my therapy,
I was in such a bad place, no fault of my own,
Constant abuse, my mind was just blown.

Find the proper help, it just takes a while
But that's ok, I'm still here and now I can smile.

I love laughing
I love my family
I love my friends
I love my dogs
I love fishing/hunting
I love gardening

I love canning
I love smiling

I LOVE LIFE

It's been one heck of a journey but I made it.
Now onto my next chapter.

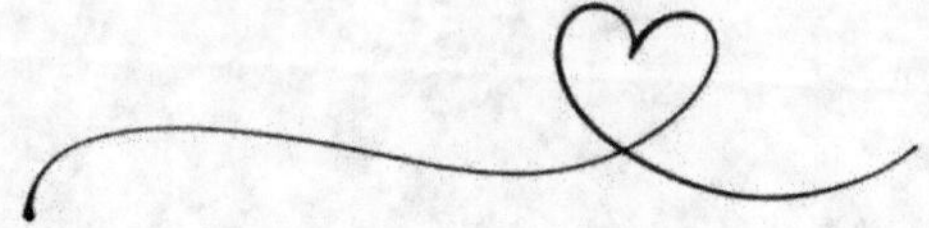

CUP OF TEA

This cool Mad Hatter asked me
Would you like a cup of tea
Well, I need something stronger
For my mind to be set free
He said, add some little magic
And then you will see . . .
This most beautiful world
In your crystal clarity.
So I took a little sip . . .
Now . . . .
This is where I want to be
That fluffy white rabbit
Bouncing circles all around me.

Magical Madness

MAGIC

If you do not believe in magic
Nothing magical will happen for you

So true

Trish - 2023